MISTER TITANIC

A Play by John Townsend

Series Editors: Steve Barlow and Steve Skidmore

Heinemann

Published by Heinemann Educational Publishers
Halley Court, Jordan Hill, Oxford OX2 8EJ
A division of Reed Educational and Professional Publishing Ltd

OXFORD   MELBOURNE   AUCKLAND
JOHANNESBURG   BLANTYRE   GABORONE
IBADAN   PORTSMOUTH NH (USA)   CHICAGO

© John Townsend, 2001
Original illustrations © Heinemann Educational Publishers 2001

First published 2001
05 04 03 02 01
10   9   8   7   6   5   4   3   2   1
ISBN 0 435 21284 2

Illustrations by Carlos Pino
Cover Design by Shireen Nathoo Design
Cover image from the Moviestore Collection
Designed by Artistix, Thame, Oxon
Printed and bound in Great Britain by Biddles Ltd

Tel: 01865 888058 www.heinemann.co.uk

Contents

Characters   4

Scene One   7

Scene Two   16

Scene Three   25

Characters

LEO is an out-of-work actor who thinks he is terrific.
He can't act at all! He dreams of being a star.

MUM is Leo's mother. She is fed up with him doing nothing.

KATE is another actor who isn't very good. She gets upset very easily and is rather moody.

TROY is the director of a play called 'Titanic'. His hair and clothes are very bright.

DJ is a smooth and flashy radio disc-jockey.

Smaller Parts

MICHAEL is the host of 'This Is Your Life'.

DALE is a TV chat show host.

DES is another TV chat show host.

If you perform the play:
KATE and **MUM** can be played by one person. **DJ**, **MICHAEL**, **DALE**, **TROY**, and **DES** can be played by one person.

SCENE ONE

LEO: It isn't easy being a superstar. Girls throw themselves at me all day. That can be tricky, in the middle of Asda.

(His mobile rings. He picks it up.)

LEO: Hi, Kate. Sorry, I can't talk now. I'm about to go on air.

(He puts his mobile down.)

It's yet another chat show …

(He starts to daydream and DJ appears in a flash of lights.)

DJ: Hi there, Leo. It's good of you to drop in to the studio. So what's your latest film?

LEO: A blockbuster set on an island.

DJ: Cool! Sounds great. More pretty girls?

LEO: Hundreds.

DJ: Cool! And how much do you get for starring in this one?

LEO: Ten million dollars.

DJ: Cool! Will you get an Oscar for this?

LEO: Sure. I'm great in it.

DJ: Cool! Any plans for your next movie?

LEO: Sure. It's 'Titanic – The Return'.

DJ: Real cool! Wow, tell me more.

LEO: This time it's the iceberg that sinks – with all penguins on deck.

(There is sudden knocking. DJ disappears and Leo snaps out of his dream.)

MUM: *(She pokes her head round the door)* Leo! Are you there? Are you daydreaming again? I need your socks and pants for the wash. Hurry up!

LEO: Yeah ... alright, Mum. In a minute. I'm busy. Just getting ready.

MUM: Getting ready? The only thing you're getting ready for is the dole. All you do is daydream of being a star. What good is that? *(She exits.)*

LEO: Yeah, well ... one day.

(He flicks back his hair, starts dreaming, and Michael appears with a big red book.)

MICHAEL: Leonardo DiPatio?

LEO: Yeah, that's me.

MICHAEL: Of 32 Brick Drive?

LEO: Sure. What can I do for you?

MICHAEL: Are you the famous model, actor, superstar and sex symbol?

LEO: That's right.

MICHAEL: Then hold it right there. The car's waiting. The crowds are cheering. Come with me ...

LEO: Hey ... is it ... no, it can't be. It's Michael ...

MICHAEL: Because tonight, Leonardo DiPatio ...

LEO: I don't believe it!

MICHAEL: THIS IS YOUR LIFE! *(Music.)*

LEO: This is amazing.

MICHAEL: You were a born actor from the start.

LEO: Oh no, don't say you've got pictures of me as a fairy at infant school?

MICHAEL: Oh yes. And who better to tell us all about it than your own stunning mother …

(Michael disappears as Mum barges in with duster, mop and bucket.)

MUM: Oy! I haven't got all day, you know. Why have you got sunglasses on? I bet you're dreaming again. Get real, Leonard. Get a life. And – do something *useful!*

LEO: One day this face will be famous.

MUM: Not with those spots. Eat more greens.

LEO: I'll be a fine actor one day. I've already done well as a model.

MUM: True. I'm very proud of you. I keep the picture by my bed. A shame it's just your feet on page six of the Kay's Catalogue.

LEO: My feet have sold lots of trainers. My agent said my feet will go far. He said one day my face will be spotted.

MUM: It already is. It's covered with spots. You should put cream on them. And eat your greens. You won't get a part in a film looking like that, Leonard.

LEO: Not Leonard. It's Leonardo DiPatio now.

MUM: DiPatio? Is that because all you do is sit about? Patios are for sitting about on. Even your bone idle brother's had a better film career than you!

LEO: He's never been in films!

MUM: He works on the photo counter at Boots.

LEO: Well, I've already been on TV.

MUM: Only when you went in the bank. They got you on camera looking shifty.

LEO: I thought I looked great on 'Crimewatch'. One day I'll get my face in the paper.

MUM: That's what worries me. 'Hopeless Actor Shot By Mother'.

LEO: It just so happens I've been asked to be in a play next week. It could be my chance to make the big time.

MUM: Let's hope so. You need some money to buy new socks. It smells in here.

LEO: It's a big part. The WI are doing a Titanic evening at the scout hut. I think I'll go down very well.

MUM: Just like the Titanic did! You know I love you to bits, son. But you'll have to get a real job soon. Now, pick up those socks and stop daydreaming. *(She exits.)*

(Leo's mobile rings. He answers.)

LEO: Hi … hello, Troy … Yeah, I know all my words for 'Titanic' … Fine. I'll come down for a rehearsal when I get back from the BBC … Bye.

(He puts down his mobile and starts to daydream. Dale appears in a flashy jacket.)

DALE: And tonight on my show, it's great to welcome the one and only … please stop screaming, girls … Leonardo DiPatio …

(Music and screams.)

LEO: Hi, Dale.

DALE: Great to have you here. You look terrific.

LEO: Yeah – no spots thanks to my mum!

DALE: Your mum must be so proud of you, Leo.

LEO: You bet. But there was a time when she didn't think I'd make the big time.

DALE: And she lives with you in Hollywood?

LEO: Yeah – she washes all my socks.

DALE: Tell us about when you hit the big time.

LEO: 'Titanic'. I played the part of Jack at the scout hut. I was so good. They begged me to go to Hollywood.

DALE: And the rest, as they say, is history!

LEO: That's right. I've made tons of films now. I need a bodyguard to keep all the girls off me.

DALE: *All* the girls?

LEO: *(With a wink)* Well, maybe not *all*.

(The door opens. Mum barges in. Dale disappears.)

MUM: There's a girl to see you. She's in the kitchen. I told her you're busy daydreaming and putting cream on your spots.

LEO: Thanks! Who is she?

MUM: Her name's Kate. She's got spots, too.

LEO: She's in the play with me. I'll get my script and bag. It looks like I'm off to work. The Titanic calls! *(He exits.)*

MUM: *(Calling after him)* Work? I worry about you. All you can do is daydream. This play won't get you far. We all know what became of the Titanic.

(Blackout.)

SCENE TWO

The scout hut, an hour later. Troy writes on his clipboard as Leo and Kate stand on the stage.

TROY: *(Clapping)* Okay, okay, okay. Super. Gather round. Time to make a start. I hope you know your words, dears.

LEO: Like the back of my hand.

KATE: That's because you've got half the script written on it!

LEO: A trick I picked up at drama school.

KATE: Really? I was trained to learn my words. I know all mine back to front.

LEO: Very clever! In that case we'll have to start at the end.

KATE: *(Shouting)* Is that meant to be funny?

TROY: Okay. Okay. Let's all be friends. Let's relax. Deep breathing. Fill those lungs. Stretch. Big breaths. And relax.

KATE: Now you've started my asthma.

TROY: We're going to start with your first scene. It's where Jack and Rose first meet on the deck of Titanic. You need to be very upset, Kate.

KATE: That will be very easy. I thought this was going to be a proper play – with proper actors.

LEO:	And what do you mean by that?
KATE:	And not with a halfwit who has words on his hands and spots on his face.
LEO:	You're a one to talk!
KATE:	How dare you!
TROY:	Now now. Let's relax. Let's be calm. Let's start to act, shall we?
KATE:	I happen to be very good, you know. They even said they want to try me on 'The Weakest Link'.
LEO:	You won't need to try very hard! Let's face it, you're the weakest link for miles. Goodbye!
TROY:	Please! Please! Just relax. After all, you have to fall in love.
KATE:	I'm not doing the love scene with him! I'd never kiss that face.
TROY:	Please! Please! Can we start? Just put on that hat, Kate.
KATE:	I hate hats. They don't suit me.

LEO: That one will. It'll hide your face.

KATE: That's it! I'm not going to act with this ... with this ... with this ...

LEO: Forgotten your words?

KATE: Aaaaah! *(She storms off.)*

TROY: Oh dear. And we were all getting on so well. Try to be kind to her, Leo. Now, please get into your part. Jack has to be nice and jolly.

LEO: No problem.

TROY: And Irish.

LEO: Easy.

TROY: Okay. Good. Super. So are we ready? You just walk on, Kate. Kate, hello?

KATE: Yes. *(She walks on crying.)*

TROY: Great! Rose is upset as she enters. She goes to the rail of the ship and climbs over. She wants to end it all.

KATE: I know how she feels.

TROY: Look down into the sea and wipe a tear from your eye. You're about to jump when Jack walks on. Go.

LEO: *(Over-acting badly)* Don't do it!!

KATE: *(Also over-acting)* Stay back.

LEO: Take my hand! I'll pull you in!

KATE: No. Stay there! I'll jump.

LEO: No. DON'T!

TROY: Stop! Stop. What are you doing?

LEO: Acting.

TROY: Leo, your voice has changed. You sound like you've come off the set of 'Eastenders'. Give it bounce. Say your line, Kate.

KATE: Don't tell me what to do!

TROY: But it's my job, dear. I'm the boss.

KATE: *(To Troy)* I was acting. It's my line.

TROY: Oh – right. Yes, I see. Very good.

LEO: *(Reading off his hand and hopping)* Take my hand!

KATE: *(She snaps at Leo angrily)* I can't – you're reading from it!

TROY: Stop! Leo, why did you hop then?

LEO: It was a bounce. You said you wanted bounce.

TROY: In your voice, dear. Try again.

LEO: *(They begin again and Leo's accent changes)* Take my hand!

KATE: Go away!

LEO: *(He whispers angrily. He is not acting now)* No need to be nasty.

KATE: *(She also whispers. She's not acting either)* I was acting!

LEO: Oh, right!. *(He starts acting again)* I'll have to jump in after you.

KATE: You must be mad!

LEO: I can swim.

TROY: Take off your jacket.

(Leo takes off his jacket.)

KATE: The fall will kill you!

TROY: Your shoes. Start taking off your shoes.

(Leo takes off his shoes.)

LEO: Sure, it will hurt! But it's that icy water that bothers me.

TROY: Start to undo your shirt.

LEO: *(To Troy)* I thought this was 'Titanic', not 'The Full Monty'!

TROY: Move closer. Now down on one knee.

LEO: *(Acting)* I once went fishing as a kid ...

TROY: Lower. Much lower.

LEO: *(Making his voice as deep as he can)* I fell under the ice and almost died ...

TROY: Not your voice! You! Get down lower.

KATE: *(Acting)* You're mad!

LEO: Me mad? You're the one hanging off the back of a ship!

TROY: Socks. Take off your socks.

LEO: Must I?

KATE: *(Holding her mouth)* Oh no!

TROY: Is it your asthma, Kate?

KATE: *(To Troy)* That smell. It's his socks!

TROY: Jump ship! Women and children first!

KATE: Just a minute! Those feet. I know those feet.

LEO: Really?

KATE: Page six of the Kay's Catalogue.

LEO: Wow – am I so famous?

KATE: Yes. I've got those feet on my wall. I'd know them anywhere. Maybe I like you after all!

LEO: But – how come?

KATE: Simple. The legs on page seven. They're mine. My ankles have sold socks all over the world.

TROY: I wish you'd sell some new ones to Leo!

KATE: You and I are side by side in the Kay's Catalogue. We must be made for each other! We belong together! I love you after all!
(She kisses him.)

TROY: At last. REAL ACTING!

(Blackout.)

Scene Three

A few weeks later back in Leo's bedroom. Leo lies on the bed reading his 'Titanic' script. Mum hoovers around him. They shout above the noise.

LEO: Mum, I've got a new girlfriend.

MUM: Move these socks. I'm trying to hoover.

LEO: Did you hear me?

MUM: What?

LEO: I said I've got a girlfriend.

MUM: *(Switching off the hoover)* Sorry, love, I can't hear a word. For a funny moment I thought you said you had a girlfriend.

LEO: That's right. It's Kate.

MUM: Kate Winslet, I suppose. Here we go again. I wish you'd stop all this dreaming.

LEO: I mean it. She came here the other day.

MUM: Oh, *her*.

LEO: And she's got me a job. Her dad's in drugs.

MUM: You're not getting mixed up in that sort of thing. I thought she looked odd.

LEO: No – he works for Superdrug. He said they've been looking for a face like mine for years. I'm already famous.

MUM: Here we go again. You're living in cloud cuckoo land. Get real, Leonard.

LEO: We have to do a love scene.

MUM: Now you are dreaming! Not in those socks!

LEO: No – in the play. In fact, can I use your vacuum cleaner for the scene?

MUM: For a love scene? Whatever for?

LEO: It says so – here in my script.

MUM: Where?

LEO: It says, 'While Kate brushes her hair, Leo hoovers in the background.'

MUM: Really? Show me that script. *(She reads the page he shows her)* It says, 'Leo *hovers* in the background.'

LEO: I thought it seemed odd!

MUM: You do make me laugh, Leonard! Why don't you try and get out more, love? You can come out with me to judo.

LEO: Don't you mean bingo?

MUM: Oh no, I gave that up. Judo is much better. The prizes aren't so good but I get to throw lots of men about.

LEO: I can't go out now. That's the cost of fame.

MUM: Don't start that dreaming again. Look at this room, it's a tip. I'll get a paper to put under those muddy boots. *(She exits.)*

(Leo dreams. Lights. Music. Des appears.)

DES: And tonight on my show, I'm pleased to welcome that famous couple who are never off the screen. They're never out of the papers ... and they're never out of work. Ladies and gentlemen, give a big hand for tonight's guests: Leo and Kate!

(Kate enters and sits next to Leo.)

KATE: Hi, Des.

LEO: Hi, Des.

DES: It's great to have you both here. The famous Mister and Miss Titanic! After all, your faces are known all over the country. You can't go out without being spotted, can you?

KATE: That's an old joke, Des.

LEO: I'm always signing autographs.

DES: We've all seen you. You're everywhere. You're on the posters all over town. You're in all the glossy magazines. How does that feel?

KATE: Great.

DES: And is it true you're really in love?

(Slushy music. They hold hands and look lovingly into each other's eyes.)

KATE: Always. Forever.

(Cheers. Lights off. Kate disappears. Mum enters with a newspaper. She opens it, puts it down on the floor and stares.)

MUM: Look! In the paper. It's you. It's you and that Kate. A double-page spread. My son! I don't believe it. You're famous!

LEO: Yeah – and I hate it.

MUM: *(Reading from the paper)* 'Try new Titanic Spot Cream. See your spots go down without a trace.'

LEO: Don't remind me! It was all Kate's dad's idea. His company made a brand new skin cream. He said I was just right for all the adverts.

MUM: *(Still reading)* 'Leonardo DiPatio is the new face of the millennium. There are no spots on him! Try new Titanic Cream and see those pimples sink!'

LEO: It's so cheesy!

MUM: Leo, you're a star! You've made it! I'm so proud of you. This is it! Why didn't you tell me? Come on, we're going out on the town!

LEO: Where? Where are we going?

MUM: We're off to buy you some new socks for a start. *(Kissing him)* You lovely boy! I always knew you'd do it. I knew you'd make the big time one day. I knew those drama classes would be the making of you. Like I always said: Your acting knocks spots off everyone else!

(Blackout.)